PRIMARY SOURCES OF
FAMOUS PEOPLE IN AMERICAN HISTORY™

BENJAMIN FRANKLIN

EARLY AMERICAN GENIUS

MAYA GLASS

rosen central
Primary Source™

The Rosen Publishing Group, Inc., New York

Published in 2004 by The Rosen Publishing Group, Inc.
29 East 21st Street, New York, NY 10010

Copyright © 2004 by The Rosen Publishing Group, Inc.

First Edition

Library of Congress Cataloging-in-Publication Data

Glass, Maya.
Benjamin Franklin : early American genius / by Maya Glass.
    v. cm. — (Primary sources of Famous people in American history)
Contents: Benjamin Franklin the apprentice — A struggle and a success — Printer and citizen — Benjamin Franklin the inventor — Benjamin Franklin, great American.
ISBN 0-8239-4103-5 (lib. bdg.)
ISBN 0-8239-4175-2 (pbk)
6-pack 0-8239-4302-X
1. Franklin, Benjamin, 1706–1790—Juvenile literature. 2. Statesmen—United States—Biography—Juvenile literature. 3. Inventors—United States—Biography—Juvenile literature. 4. Printers—United States—Biography—Juvenile literature. 5. Scientists—United States—Biography—Juvenile literature. [1. Franklin, Benjamin, 1706–1790. 2. Statesmen. 3. Scientists. 4. Inventors. 5. Printers.] I. Title. II. Series.
E302.6.F8 G55 2003
973.3'092—dc21

                                                    2002155679

Manufactured in the United States of America

Photo credits: cover © Francis G. Mayer/Corbis; p. 4 © Bettmann/Corbis; p. 5 © National Portrait Gallery, Smithsonian Institution/Art Resource, NY; pp. 6, 10 courtesy of the Rare Books and Manuscripts Collection, The New York Public Library, Astor, Lenox, and Tilden Foundations; p. 7 Dover Pictorial Archive Series; p. 11 The American Philosophical Society; p. 12 New-York Historical Society, New York, USA/Bridgeman Art Library; pp. 13, 17, 26, 27, 29 Library of Congress Prints and Photographs Division; pp. 15, 25 © Hulton/Archive/Getty Images, p. 19 Cigna Museum and Art Collection; pp. 20, 21 Franklin Institute; p. 23 Archives Charmet/The Bridgeman Art Library; p. 28 National Archives and Records Administration.

Designer: Thomas Forget; Photo Researcher: Rebecca Anguin-Cohen

CONTENTS

1 BENJAMIN FRANKLIN THE APPRENTICE

Benjamin Franklin was born on January 17, 1706, in Boston, Massachusetts. Benjamin was the fifteenth of seventeen children. When he was eight, he went to school. He did not stay long in school because his family needed him to work. Benjamin became an apprentice to his father at age ten.

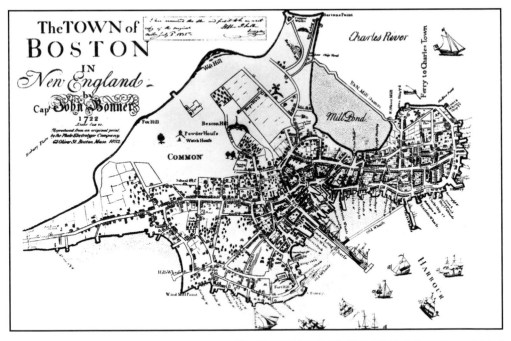

Boston was the largest city in New England in 1706. Ships coming from Europe helped the city become rich.

Benjamin Franklin left school before the age of ten. He never stopped learning, though. He always read books and used his mind.

5

Benjamin learned how to make soap and candles. Benjamin did not like the work. He liked reading better. He then became an apprentice to his brother James. They worked as printers. Printers are people who make newspapers and books for people to read.

Boys who didn't go to school started working early in life. They usually became apprentices in a trade. Apprentices are helpers who learn a business.

Printing shops in colonial times were small. They often
printed newspapers, pamphlets, or advertising leaflets.
Printing took skill and was learned over many years.

James Franklin started his own newspaper in 1721. Benjamin wanted to write for the paper. James thought his brother was too young to write well. Benjamin wrote articles using a different name, Mrs. Silence Dogood. The articles made fun of the Puritans in Boston. Sometimes Benjamin took over the printing.

DID YOU KNOW?

Benjamin Franklin was a vegetarian. He ate only vegetables and bread. He did not eat any meat.

THE
New-England Courant.

From MONDAY April 9. to MONDAY April 16. 1722.

To the Author of the New-England Courant.

SIR, [N° 2

HISTORIES of Lives are seldom entertaining, unless they contain something either admirable or exemplar: And since there is little or nothing of this Nature in my own Adventures, I will not tire your Readers with tedious Particulars of no Consequence, but will briefly, and in as few Words as possible, relate the most material Occurrences of my Life, and according to my Promise, confine all to this Letter.

MY Reverend Master who had hitherto remained a Batchelor, (after much Meditation on the Eighteenth verse of the Second Chapter of Genesis,) took up a Resolution to marry; and having made several unsuccessful fruitless Attempts on the more topping Sort of our Sex, and being tir'd with making troublesome Journeys and Visits to no Purpose, he began unexpectedly to cast a loving Eye upon Me, whom he had brought up cleverly to his Hand.

THERE is certainly scarce any Part of a Man's Life in which he appears more silly and ridiculous, than when he makes his first Onset in Courtship. The awkward Manner in which my Master first discover'd his Intentions, made me, in spite of my Reverence to his Person, burst out into an unmannerly Laughter: However, having ask'd his Pardon, and with much ado compos'd my Countenance, I promis'd him I would take his Proposal into serious Consideration, and speedily give him an Answer.

AS he had been a great Benefactor (and in a Manner a Father to me) I could not well deny his Request, when I once perceived he was in earnest. Whether it was Love, or Gratitude, or Pride, or all Three that made me consent, I know not; but it is certain, he found it no hard Matter, by the Help of his Rhetorick, to conquer my Heart, and perswade me to marry him.

THIS unexpected Match was very astonishing to all the Country round about, and served to furnish

AT present I pass away my leisure Hours in Conversation, either with my honest Neighbour Rusticus and his Family, or with the ingenious Minister of our Town, who now lodges at my House, and by whose Assistance I intend now and then to beautify my Writings with a Sentence or two in the learned Languages, which will not only be fashionable, and pleasing to those who do not understand it, but will likewise be very ornamental.

I SHALL conclude this with my own Character, which (one would think) I should be best able to give. Know then, That I am an Enemy to Vice, and a Friend to Virtue. I am one of an extensive Charity, and a great Forgiver of private Injuries: A hearty Lover of the Clergy and all good Men, and a mortal Enemy to arbitrary Government & unlimited Power. I am naturally very jealous for the Rights and Liberties of my Country; & the least appearance of an Incroachment on those invaluable Priviledges, is apt to make my Blood boil exceedingly. I have likewise a natural Inclination to observe and reprove the Faults of others, at which I have an excellent Faculty. I speak this by Way of Warning to all such whose Offences shall come under my Cognizance, for I never intend to wrap my Talent in a Napkin. To be brief; I am courteous and affable, good-humour'd (unless I am first provok'd,) and handsome, and sometimes witty, but always,

SIR,
Your Friend, and
Humble Servant,
SILENCE DOGOOD.

To the Author of the New-England Courant.
SIR,

BEing lately at the Quarter-Sessions, when a certain Lawyer came upon his Tryal for cohabiting with a French Taylor's as his Wife without being married according to the Laws of this Province, it was with no small Indignation that I heard him deliver himself to this Purpose; 'Please your Honours, I have been render'd odious by a Company of scandalous Writers, which I need not wonder at, when even his Excellency himself, and all that is dear and sacred to your Honours, has not escap'd the Lash of these sorry Scribblers: And since the Town are so much byas'd by their Writings, I chuse not to be try'd by

Ben Franklin was only sixteen when he began to write essays in the *New-England Courant*. He often wrote about the importance of living a good life.

2 A STRUGGLE AND A SUCCESS

Benjamin Franklin moved to New York in 1723. He was seventeen years old. He did not find work there. A printer told him to try Philadelphia. In Philadelphia, Franklin worked with the printer Samuel Keimer. During this time, Franklin met Deborah Read. She would later become his wife. Franklin wanted to start his own printing shop.

Ben Franklin wanted to start his own print shop. He didn't have much luck at first. He moved to Philadelphia and soon met his future wife, Deborah Read.

Deborah Read saw quickly that Franklin was smart and witty. She also liked that he had high goals for his life. They wrote letters to each other and met on city streets.

Franklin had no money to start his own shop. He sailed to London to try getting loans. He needed equipment. He did not have much luck. He went to work as a teacher. In 1726, he went back to Philadelphia to work again with Samuel Keimer. In 1728, Franklin opened a printing shop with Hugh Meredith.

A SECRET AUTHOR

Benjamin Franklin also wrote newspaper articles using the name Busy Body.

Ben Franklin used this printing press in his Philadelphia print shop. Printing was slow work. Only one page at a time could be printed.

3 PRINTER AND CITIZEN

In 1729, Benjamin Franklin bought Samuel Keimer's newspaper, the *Pennsylvania Gazette*. People loved to read Franklin's lively writing. The paper sold well in Philadelphia. In 1730, Franklin and Deborah Read were married by common law. Common law meant they had lived together long enough to be considered married.

Franklin managed his print shop closely. He read everything that was printed. He wanted only the best-written stories printed in his newspaper.

THE
Pennsylvania GAZETTE.

Numb. XL.

Containing the freshest Advices Foreign and Domestick.

From Thursday, September 25. to Thursday, October 2. 1729.

THE Pennsylvania Gazette being now to be carry'd on by other Hands, the Reader may expect some Account of the Method we design to proceed in.

Upon a View of Chambers's great Dictionaries, from whence were taken the Materials of the Universal Instructor in all Arts and Sciences, which usually made the First Part of this Paper, we find that besides their containing many Things abstruse or insignificant to us, it will probably be fifty Years before the Whole can be gone thro' in this Manner of Publication. There are likewise in those Books continual References from Things under one Letter of the Alphabet to those under another, which relate to the same Subject, and are necessary to explain and compleat it; these taken in their Turn may perhaps be Ten Years distant; and since it is likely that they who desire to acquaint themselves with any particular Art or Science, would gladly have the whole before them in a much less Time, we believe our Readers will not think such a Method of communicating Knowledge to be a proper One.

However, tho' we do not intend to continue the Publication of those Dictionaries in a regular Alphabetical Method, as has hitherto been done; yet as several Things exhibited from them in the Course of these Papers, have been entertaining to such of the Curious, who never had and cannot have the Advantage of good Libraries; and as there are many Things still behind, which being in this Manner made generally known, may perhaps become of considerable Use, by giving such Hints to the excellent natural Genius's of our Country, as may contribute either to the Improvement of our present Manufactures, or towards the Invention of new Ones; we propose from Time to Time to communicate such particu-

There are many who have long desired to see a good News-Paper in Pennsylvania; and we hope those Gentlemen who are able, will contribute towards the making This such. We ask Assistance, because we are fully sensible, that to publish a good News-Paper is not so easy an Undertaking as many People imagine it to be. The Author of a Gazette (in the Opinion of the Learned) ought to be qualified with an extensive Acquaintance with Languages, a great Easiness and Command of Writing and Relating Things cleanly and intelligibly, and in few Words; he should be able to speak of War both by Land and Sea; be well acquainted with Geography, with the History of the Time, with the several Interests of Princes and States, the Secrets of Courts, and the Manners and Customs of all Nations. Men thus accomplish'd are very rare in this remote Part of the World; and it would be well if the Writer of these Papers could make up among his Friends what is wanting in himself.

Upon the Whole, we may assure the Publick, that as far as the Encouragement we meet with will enable us, no Care and Pains shall be omitted, that may make the Pennsylvania Gazette as agreeable and useful an Entertainment as the Nature of the Thing will allow.

The Following is the last Message sent by his Excellency Governour Burnet, to the House of Representatives in Boston.

Gentlemen of the House of Representatives,

IT is not with so vain a Hope as to convince you, that I take the Trouble to answer your Messages, but, if possible, to open the Eyes of the deluded People whom you represent, and whom you are at so much Pains to keep in Ignorance of the true State of their Affairs. I need no

---

The *Pennsylvania Gazette* came out once each week. The newspaper was just a few pages long. People often bought a single paper and passed it around to family and friends.

Benjamin Franklin's *Poor Richard's Almanack* came out in 1732. An almanac is a book that has recipes and information such as weather reports. Farmers use it to help them know when to plant their crops. The printing shop went so well that Franklin hired help. He wanted to spend more time on science and politics.

PRINTING MONEY

Benjamin Franklin used his printing press to print paper money for the government.

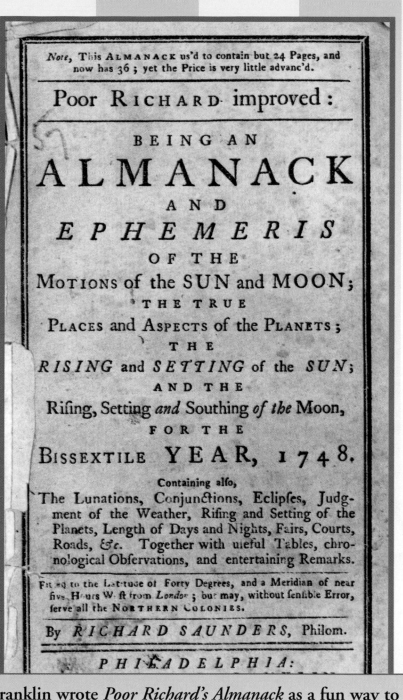

Note, This ALMANACK us'd to contain but 24 Pages, and now has 36; yet the Price is very little advanc'd.

Poor RICHARD improved:

BEING AN

ALMANACK

AND

EPHEMERIS

OF THE

Motions of the SUN and MOON;

THE TRUE

Places and Aspects of the Planets;

THE

RISING and SETTING of the SUN;

AND THE

Rising, Setting *and* Southing *of the* Moon,

FOR THE

Bissextile YEAR, 1748.

Containing also,

The Lunations, Conjunctions, Eclipses, Judgment of the Weather, Rising and Setting of the Planets, Length of Days and Nights, Fairs, Courts, Roads, &c. Together with useful Tables, chronological Observations, and entertaining Remarks.

Fitted to the Latitude of Forty Degrees, and a Meridian of near five Hours West from *London*; but may, without sensible Error, serve all the NORTHERN COLONIES.

By *RICHARD SAUNDERS*, Philom.

PHILADELPHIA:

Franklin wrote *Poor Richard's Almanack* as a fun way to help people live a good life. His short sayings showed the good that hard work could do for everyone. They also taught people how to be wise with money and time.

Franklin helped Philadelphia in many ways. Around 1740, he invented a stove that was better than the ones used at the time. He held meetings so people could talk about their ideas. He served as deputy postmaster of the colonies from 1753 to 1774. He also helped to form a fire-fighting company, a police force, and a library in Philadelphia.

A BOOK OF SAYINGS

Poor Richard's Almanack had many sayings that we still use today. One is "One bad apple spoils the bunch." Today's sayings often use different words.

Ben Franklin saw that cities needed everyone's help to work smoothly. He argued that everyone held a share in a city's safety. Franklin helped form fire and police departments in Philadelphia.

19

4 BENJAMIN FRANKLIN THE INVENTOR

Ben Franklin invented many things. He invented a stove to heat a house. He also made bifocal glasses. Bifocals are special glasses that help people see both near and far. He invented lightning rods, too. These metal rods are put on houses to protect them. Lightning hits the rods and then it goes into the ground.

One of Franklin's most useful inventions was his bifocal glasses. They helped people see more clearly. This improved people's everyday lives.

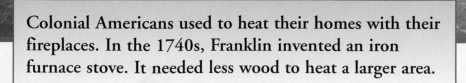

Colonial Americans used to heat their homes with their fireplaces. In the 1740s, Franklin invented an iron furnace stove. It needed less wood to heat a larger area.

21

Franklin wanted to prove that lightning was a form of electricity. It is thought that he did a lightning experiment in 1752. He flew a kite with a metal key on it. The key got hit by lightning and was filled with electricity. The electricity went from the kite to Franklin, and he felt a shock. That is how Franklin knew that lightning was electric.

DID YOU KNOW?

Benjamin Franklin liked to do puzzles. He invented a magic square, a kind of puzzle done with numbers.

FRANKLIN.

Ben Franklin had an idea that lightning was a form of electricity. He tested his theory and found out that he was right. He then invented the lightning rod to protect homes from fire caused by lightning.

23

Benjamin Franklin became a politician. He worked in London to get the British to listen to the colonies. Britain ruled the colonies during the 1700s. The colonies wanted to rule themselves. Events in America led to the American Revolution. The Stamp Act placed a tax on many printed items. The act made the colonies angry.

POLITICAL CARTOONIST

Many people think Benjamin Franklin's drawing "Join or Die" was the first political cartoon. It shows a snake that stands for the colonies cut into pieces.

American colonists in the 1770s no longer wanted to pay British taxes. Britain's harsh treatment forced colonists to revolt. This drawing shows British tax collectors fleeing from angry colonists.

The Boston Massacre happened on March 5, 1770. British soldiers shot a group of colonists who did not have guns. This made colonists hate the British even more. In 1773, Britain taxed tea. Colonists dressed as Native Americans dumped boxes of tea into Boston Harbor. This was known as the Boston Tea Party.

British tea merchants lost thousands of dollars in the Boston Tea Party. Dumping tea into the harbor showed Britain that the colonies demanded change. Soon, colonists were demanding independent rule.

British soldiers patrolled Boston and other colonial cities in the 1770s. The anger that built up during these times caused the Boston Massacre. British troops killed five colonists during the fighting.

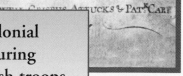

27

In 1775, Franklin returned to Philadelphia. He became a member of the Continental Congress. Thomas Jefferson wrote the Declaration of Independence in 1776. Franklin was one of the people to sign it. Benjamin Franklin worked to serve his country for the rest of his life. He died on April 17, 1790.

At left is the Declaration of Independence. It lists the reasons why the colonies wanted to split from Great Britain.

Ben Franklin was a wise old man by the time Thomas Jefferson wrote the Declaration of Independence. Franklin read the document and gave Jefferson advice on rewriting it.

TIMELINE

1706—Benjamin Franklin is born on January 17, in Boston, Massachusetts.

1722—Franklin begins writing his Silence Dogood letters.

1732—The first *Poor Richard's Almanack* is published.

1765—Franklin and others protest the Stamp Act.

1773—The Boston Tea Party happens.

1790— Franklin dies on April 17 in Philadelphia. He is 84 years old.

1718—Franklin becomes a printer's helper to his brother James.

1730—Franklin and Deborah Read are married by common law.

1737—Franklin becomes postmaster of Philadelphia.

1770—The Boston Massacre happens.

1776—Franklin reads and signs the Declaration of Independence.

GLOSSARY

apprentice (uh-PREN-tis) A person who learns a trade by working for an experienced person.

colonies (KOL-uh-neez) A territory settled by people from another country and controlled by that country.

common-law marriage (KAH-mun-LAW MAR-ij) A marriage between a man and a woman who have lived together for a certain period of time.

deputy postmaster (DEP-yoo-tee POHST-mas-ter) A person who helps to sort and deliver mail.

electricity (ih-lek-TRIH-sih-tee) Energy that makes light, heat, or motion.

equipment (uh-KWIP-mint) The materials needed to make or do something.

experiment (ek-SPER-uh-ment) A test.

politician (pah-lih-TIH-shun) A person who holds or runs for a public office.

politics (PAH-lih-tiks) The science of government and elections.

Puritans (PYUR-ih-tenz) Members of a religious group in England who moved to America during the seventeenth century.

WEB SITES

Due to the changing nature of Internet links, the Rosen Publishing Group, Inc., has developed an online list of Web sites related to the subject of this book. This site is updated regularly. Please use this link to access the list:

http://www.rosenlinks.com/fpah/bfra

PRIMARY SOURCE IMAGE LIST

Page 4: A 1722 illustrated map titled "The Town of Boston in New England" by John Bonner.

Page 5: Portrait of Benjamin Franklin by Joseph Duplessis, circa 1785. It is currently housed at the Smithsonian Institution, Washington, D.C.

Page 7: Engraving of a print shop, circa 1730, from Denis Diderot's encyclopedia of trades.

Page 9: Photograph of Ben Franklin article written for the *New-England Courant*, April 16, 1722.

Page 11: Oil painting of Deborah Franklin by Benjamin Wilson, circa 1758. It is currently housed at the American Philosophical Society, Philadelphia.

Page 13: Photograph of the printing press used by Franklin. The press is currently housed at the Smithsonian's National Museum of American History, Washington, D.C.

INDEX

ABOUT THE AUTHOR

Maya Glass is a writer and editor living in New York City.